Congratulations!

Your engagement is a happy and exciting time. The
smart couple plans for a lifetime together, not just
the wedding date. With proper thought and planning,
a prenuptial agreement (prenup) can provide you
with a great roadmap for the years to come!

For Emil, Blake, and Brett—with love.

Why the elephant?

While prenups are becoming more popular, it is sometimes difficult to know how to approach the topic. The prenup can be the elephant in the room—the idea that nobody wants to discuss. I invite you to use this handbook to explore how a prenup can help build a strong foundation for your marriage.

This book is meant to give you a general framework for how prenups operate and how the process of arriving at a prenup works. The information in this book may help you determine whether a prenup is a wise choice. It should not take the place of the information and insight your attorney can provide based upon your individual circumstances and your state's laws. Legal agreements are increasingly complex, and the details of your agreement need to be well developed and clear.

I hope you find this book useful as you make decisions about your life together!

Contents

CONTENTS

Acknowledgments

My professional choices have been based upon my strong desire to help people meet the challenges that life brings. I enjoy feeling that my work has a positive effect on the many diverse and wonderful people I meet in my practice and in my classroom.

The idea behind this book was to help people think about how they want their marital relationship to work from a financial and social perspective. I thank Kristyn Okress, Esq., for her truly invaluable assistance in the research and development of this book. Kristyn helped to make this project meaningful and fun during the many hours we spent brainstorming about how to convey the concepts in the book. Kristyn is a highly skilled attorney with a very bright future. I am also grateful to my illustrator Emily Tomasik for her amazing creativity and artistic ability. I thank my friend and colleague Michelle Brody, PhD, for sharing her thoughts on the process of writing a book.

Last, and in no way least, I want to acknowledge my husband Emil, who is my rock. He is always there for me and has been my incredible partner in every way for close to 40 years. (That includes time before and during the marriage, for those of you calculating my age!) Emil has been supportive of every project I have chosen and has kept me going through the many ups and downs of life. My wish for you is a strong partnership like mine.

CHAPTER 1

Your Journey to a Prenup Begins Here!

Create a workable plan that is unique to your situation.

I am writing this book from my perspective as a New York family lawyer and mediator. As you read, you will see that how you arrive at a final agreement is just as important as what goes into the agreement. Make sure you stay focused on the importance of maintaining a healthy relationship in reaching your goals, and allow your attorney to provide advice and counsel on your particular situation and help you navigate the prenup process.

In my own family law practice, I very often see that it is hard for people to discuss finances. This led me to think about how to address finances in a positive way early on in the marriage or even before saying "I do." Thinking and talking about expectations regarding finances and lifestyle before the marriage help to promote a healthy relationship.

There will be times throughout the book where I may give my opinion on certain courses of action or situations. My opinions (and the book in general) should not be considered legal advice. Prenups, postnuptial agreements (postnups), and no-nuptial agreements (no-nups) are contracts and, as such, are governed by contract law, which may vary from state to state. The goal here is to give you a better understanding of how the *process* of prenups actually works and to provide information so that you may make an informed decision about whether a prenup is something you would like to pursue.

Prenups should be tailored for each couple. While you may have certain issues in common with other couples, remember that the focus should always remain on you and your fiancé.[1] While reading, you might encounter examples that you may or may not want to use in creating your own prenup. The examples and suggestions are meant to encourage thinking and discussion. You and your fiancé should tailor-make your prenup to cover the elements that you *both* feel are necessary to address for your relationship.

Think about the following when discussing the prenup:

- **Be mindful of time and place.** Try to have the conversation when you are both free of distractions and can immerse yourself fully into the discussion.

- **Keep an open mind.** Acknowledge that your opinions may differ during your initial exchange of ideas. Remember that these exchanges can help align your goals for the future. You will never know unless you talk about it!

- **Remain willing and able to adapt.** While it is a good idea to plan ahead before having a prenup talk with your fiancé, remember that the conversation will undoubtedly flow in different and perhaps unanticipated directions. Allowing for flexible, honest discussions is important for both of you.

---

1. For ease in reading and consistency, "fiancé" includes both genders.

CHAPTER 2

Prenup: A Unique Plan for Your Marriage

Put your plan into effect.

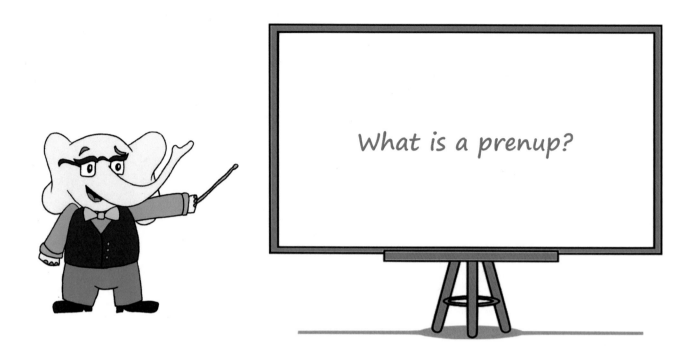

A prenup is an agreement between two parties in contemplation of marriage. It is treated as a contract that is enforceable by the courts if it meets certain requirements. A prenup takes effect upon marriage. More and more couples are entering into prenups because they are interested in communicating about financial expectations before the marriage and taking an active role in all aspects of married life. They are interested in identifying personal property and assets that were acquired prior to the marriage and protecting their rights to this property. Prenups specify all of the property each person owns or has an interest in before the marriage as well as any debt. The couple may also be interested in clarifying what will happen to property acquired during the marriage (see "Commonly included topics" on page 31).

The prenup allows the couple to arrange, in advance, financial matters in the event of separation, divorce, or death. The agreement addresses how property acquired before and during marriage will be treated. This property may include real estate, retirement, investment, and business assets. Prenups can address student and business loans, credit card debt, and support obligations. The agreement can also play a role in estate planning. In addition, the couple may want to address certain lifestyle issues.

Each couple has a unique set of goals and issues to be addressed. The content of prenups can therefore vary. Other examples of specific issues that can be addressed with a prenup are discussed throughout this book. Without a prenup, state laws dictate who owns the property that is acquired during the marriage as well as what happens upon the dissolution of the marriage. Couples that want to be proactive about the management and control of assets often consider a prenup. The agreement clarifies expectations about the couple's future life together regardless of whether there is a divorce. It can also help to avoid costly court battles over assets and finances.

While this book is focused on prenups, it should be noted that there are options available for couples who are either already married or are not able to enter into an agreement before the wedding. For example, a postnup includes the elements of a prenup and is executed after the couple is already married. There are a variety of reasons why a couple may opt for a postnup rather than a prenup. For example, perhaps there was not enough time to complete the agreement before the wedding or neither spouse wanted to bring up a stressful topic (e.g., money) amidst the wedding planning. Maybe it just never came to mind. A postnup is sometimes considered when there has been a breach of trust in the relationship and the couple wants to create certainty about what will happen in the event of a breakup. It is also a way to protect separate property used to purchase marital property.

In addition to a postnup, a couple who is not married and has no plans of marrying may enter into a no-nup (or cohabitation agreement). As the name suggests, a no-nup can provide protection for couples who prefer to stay unwed. The practice of no-nups has become more common as many couples opt to skip the wedding and build a life together without the formal ceremony. Of course, certain rights and obligations come only with marriage, and the distinguishing factors should be understood in the decision-making process.

If you're not planning to get married (at least not in the near future), and you're still interested in an agreement that establishes how finances and property ownership will be treated in your relationship, please refer to Appendix A, No-Nups (or Cohabitation Agreements), on page 93. If, on the other hand, you are already married and want to consider whether a postnup is right for you, refer to Appendix B, Postnups, on page 95.

CHAPTER 3

Working through Common Misconceptions

Balance criticism with a constructive approach: a point-counterpoint discussion.

When it comes to an opinion on prenups, there are fact-based and emotion-based opinions. In this context, emotion-based opinions are understandable and can be addressed in a productive way. The following illustrations address some of the more common misconceptions.

Wanting a prenup means that you only care about money.

The word "prenup" may trigger fearful and angry thoughts that money is more important than love: "Why are you planning for a divorce? I thought we loved each other," "Prenups are not for people like us. They are for celebrities and multimillionaires," and "Why are we talking about money now?"

NOT SO FAST!

Marriage is an economic partnership.

Marriage is a partnership in every way, including finances! Talking about money should not be looked at as a negative aspect of marriage. It should be looked at as a reality of life. It is a healthy way to keep a balanced perspective and create equality in the decision-making process. The goal is to enter the marriage with a full understanding of your situation.

"My fiancé wants a prenup.
He/she must not trust me."

A big reason that it is hard to bring up the subject of a prenup is an assumption that the person requesting the prenup lacks trust. If marriage truly is "until death," why think about a prenup?

The process can build trust and
a foundation for the future.

Discussing a prenup is a great opportunity to proactively think and talk about what will happen to property coming into the marriage as well as property acquired during the marriage. Trust is built by sharing ideas in order to have a better understanding of what will happen with or without a prenup.

"Prenups just prepare for divorce."

People are sometimes opposed to prenups because they feel that having one implies planning for a divorce. Along the same line, some people tend to think that a prenup is just plain depressing because the focus of the agreement is about the couple breaking up.

NOT SO FAST!

Prenups are about planning for the future, regardless of what may come.

Creating a prenup is about creating a road map for your future together. A prenup encourages you and your fiancé to discuss expectations about how the marriage will work and to create a plan for how to handle financial and other issues as your marriage begins.

Prenups have existed in one form or another for over 1,000 years as a way of outlining roles and responsibilities in the marriage and providing stability and certainty. There are many examples of this throughout history.[2] The point-counterpoint discussion shows that the reasons for a prenup run deep.

A failure to communicate about money can lead to feelings of mistrust. Sometimes it is not the distribution of wealth but instead the lack of communication about finances that leads to misunderstanding or feelings of inequality in the relationship. This can happen when the incomes, assets, and/or debts are disproportionate

---

2. The earliest known marriage contract dates back to approximately 440 BCE and was between the groom and his intended father-in-law. Many elements of this agreement came to be known as the Ketubah, a Jewish marriage agreement still used today. Abraham Bloch. *The Biblical and Historical Background of Jewish Customs and Ceremonies.* New York, 1980, citing Sayce and Cowley, *Aramaic Papyri Discovered at Assuan.*

    In 15th century England, it is alleged that Edward IV had one of his wives, Eleanor Butler, enter into a prenup. Later, in 1744, Elizabeth Oglethorpe of England wanted to protect her land outside of London, and thus had her husband Edward Oglethorpe enter into a prenup for this purpose. Peter Walzer. *What Every Lawyer Wanted to Know About Prenups, But Was Afraid to Ask (An American).* International Academy of Family Lawyers, IAML Online News, Issue 23, April 2013, p. 14. https://www.iafl.com/cms_media/files/iaml_online_news_issue_23.pdf.

    Prenups took time to become widely accepted in the United States. Although the agreements existed since the 1940s, courts rarely upheld these contracts, holding instead that while women could contract, they still could not contract with and sue their husbands. The rationale behind this was that marriage was thought to make two parties become one. It wasn't until around the 1970s that prenups gained acceptance from the courts, namely because of an increase in divorces. Rondal B. Stadler, "Prenuptial and Postnuptial Contract Law in the United States," 2008. http://www.rbs2.com/dcontract.pdf.

or unknown coming into the marriage or when only one person knows about the assets and debt during the marriage. It can also happen when both parties are secure in their finances but fail to communicate about expectations in the marital relationship. There are many components to a happy and healthy relationship. The point-counterpoint examples address how to work through the misconceptions that can undermine prenup negotiations.

Marriages can thrive in a variety of ways. The process of discussing and potentially having a prenup affords you and your fiancé an opportunity to talk about and evaluate your thoughts and ideas when it comes to decision-making (and other responsibilities). The prenup process can provide a great platform for coming to a compromise and having a better understanding of each other's philosophies about money and expectations about the marital relationship.

CHAPTER 4

Reasons to Get a Prenup

Protect your relationship.

Marriage brings financial rights and responsibilities. It is wise to go into marriage understanding these rights and responsibilities. If you are at a prenup moment in your life, you have the ability to make choices about what happens to your property during the marriage, in the case of divorce, or in the event of death.

Although prenups may not be for everyone, the discussions about the economics of your relationship and other important issues related to the marriage *can* be useful for everyone. Whether or not a prenup is a good choice for you and your fiancé is something that you must ultimately decide on your own. Every couple has its own priorities and circumstances. Take a look at the list entitled "Commonly included topics" on page 31, which contains information about what can be included in a prenup. This could help you think about why you might want a prenup. You may also want to review the worksheet in Appendix D, Goals, on page 111. Think about your priorities and goals, and discuss your ideas with your fiancé. This also sets the stage for how you will communicate in the future.

Here are some reasons why you may want a prenup:

- **Past:** How do you want to treat the property and debt that you have already acquired?

- **Present:** How will the household income and expenses be managed?

- **Future:** How will you treat money or property that comes into the marriage?

There are numerous reasons for a prenup. To help you think about your own prenup, here is a list of topics commonly included in prenup agreements.

"Crossing that bridge when you get to it" may be the easy way to think about family life, but it is not always the smartest plan.

Commonly included topics

- Distinction between separate and marital property

- Ability to keep family property in the family

- A business or business interests acquired before/during the marriage

- Savings acquired before/during the marriage

- Retirement benefits before/during the marriage

- Apartment or house bought before/during the marriage

- Responsibility of premarital debt

- Division of property upon a divorce

- Distribution of property upon death (must be consistent with your will and other documents designating beneficiaries)

- Management of household bills and expenses during the marriage

- Management of joint bank accounts during the marriage, if any

- Acquisition and management of credit card expenditures during the marriage

- Management of financial obligations during the marriage

- Financial decisions for postmarital education

- State law to be applied

- Resolution of disputes about the prenup

- Sunset clause (i.e., if the prenup will end based upon being married for a certain number of years or if certain changes in the terms of the agreement will take place)
- Lifestyle issues or issues unique to the parties

After viewing the above list, you may want to learn more about why these topics are considered for inclusion in prenups. Sometimes the reason why people want a prenup boils down to wanting to feel a certain fairness or security in knowing what will happen as they enter the marriage. That certainty may have to do with property acquired before the marriage or how income will be considered after the marriage.

There may be only one reason considered for a prenup, such as protecting one piece of property bought by family, or several reasons. It is recommended that you consult with an attorney to determine how issues that are important to you would likely be addressed, according to relevant law, if there is no prenup. Your attorney will help you consider options for how to incorporate the terms into the document that are important to you.

Property acquired before marriage

A major reason why people opt for prenups is to protect property, such as a house or apartment purchased prior to the marriage. Another reason is to protect retirement assets or an interest in a business. Property acquired before marriage, inherited property, gifts received by a party from a third party, and passive appreciation on a premarital asset are considered separate property.[3] In general, marital property is property earned or acquired during the marriage by earnings from employment or self-employment. Under certain situations, separate property can be characterized as marital property. A consultation with an experienced family law or matrimonial attorney is helpful to clarify the law on separate and marital property (and where your own property may fall).[4]

Property acquired during marriage

With respect to marital property in states such as New York, where equitable distribution is the method for dividing a married couple's property when they divorce, unless the parties have agreed on the disposition of their marital property, in writing, the court considers factors such as the following list in determining the equitable distribution of property. (Equitable distribution does not necessarily mean equal.[5])

- Each spouse's income and property when they married and when they file for divorce

---

3. The definition of separate property under New York law can be found at DRL Sec. 236 B(1)(d).

4. The definition of marital property under New York law can be found at DRL Sec. 236 B(1)(c).

5. The equitable distribution law can be found in New York Domestic Relations Law Section 236, Part B.

- The duration of the marriage

- Each person's age and health

- The need of a custodial parent to occupy or own the family home and to use or own its household effects (e.g., furniture)

- The pension, health insurance, and inheritance rights that either spouse will lose as a result of divorce

- Whether the court has awarded maintenance (i.e., alimony)

- Whether either spouse has an equitable claim to marital property to which that spouse does not have title, based on that spouse's contribution of labor, money, or efforts as a spouse, parent, wage earner, or homemaker, including contributions to the other spouse's earning potential (e.g., working to put the other spouse through school)[6]

- The liquid or nonliquid character of all marital property

- The probable future financial circumstances of each spouse

- The impossibility or difficulty of evaluating any component asset or any interest in a business, corporation, or profession, and the economic desirability of retaining such asset or interest intact and free from any claim or interference by the other spouse

- The tax consequences to each spouse

- Whether either spouse has wastefully dissipated assets

- Whether either spouse has transferred or encumbered marital property made in contemplation of a matrimonial action without fair consideration

- Any other factor that the court shall expressly find to be a just and proper consideration

Certain assets acquired during the marriage may be considered marital property regardless of the name in which title is held. The prenup can define marital property in accordance with relevant state law or can set forth a different agreement for what constitutes marital property and how it will be distributed in the event of divorce or death. For example, the agreement may state that all property acquired after the marriage date is presumed to be marital, or it may state that only property held in joint title will be considered marital. It may also provide information about what happens if separate property is used for the purchase of property during the marriage. The agreement can specify how rights in assets acquired during the marriage will be

---

6.   NY DRL 236 B (5) (d) (7) has been amended to provide the following: "The court shall not consider as marital property subject to distribution the value of a spouse's enhanced earning capacity arising from a license, degree, celebrity goodwill, or career enhancement." As a caveat to this amendment, the new legislation states that, in determining equitable distribution, the court shall consider a spouse's direct or indirect contributions during the marriage towards the other spouse's development of enhanced earning capacity. Your attorney can advise you on how this may affect your situation. The law may be different in your state.

apportioned, or it can provide that rights in these assets are reserved and will be determined at a later date by either mutual agreement or a court of competent jurisdiction. Without such an agreement, state law dictates the distribution of property, which may not be consistent with the couple's wishes.

Second (or third) marriage

A prenup may be a wise choice if you have been previously married and have obligations or responsibilities based upon a prior relationship. For example, if you have children from a prior marriage, a prenup can be used to preserve a home or other assets for the children.

If you are currently responsible for maintenance payments or child support from a previous marriage or relationship, you will want to be sure that your obligations are fully explained to your new spouse. This helps create realistic expectations about finances. Any preexisting obligations should be explained to your attorney so that these obligations are taken into consideration in the negotiations for a prenup.

Additionally, the prior divorce agreement or judgment may have an effect on retirement benefits. These obligations can affect the benefits available to the new spouse and should be understood so that the prenup document does not conflict with prior agreements or with your intentions.

Finally, a prenup can be used if there are no children from a prior relationship and the goal is to preserve property acquired before marriage. Other important issues are addressed in the section entitled "Platinum prenups" on page 39.

Plans to start a business or a practice

Whether your goal is to run a corporation or start your own law firm or other type of business, it is smart to have a plan for how the resulting asset will be treated. The prenup process provides an opportunity to address what happens if marital funds are used or if funding from another source is necessary. Any plan for the business should include how the earnings of the business will be treated. It is advisable to negotiate these issues in advance rather than making assumptions.

Debt acquired before marriage

It is not uncommon for individuals to have either student loan debt or credit card debt (or both) when getting married. Information on debt acquired prior to the marriage is disclosed as part of the prenup process. Failure to talk about previously acquired debt can lead to mistrust in the relationship. You and your fiancé may end up using marital income to satisfy any debt, or you may decide that each will be responsible for his or her own previously acquired debt. Your prenup can address how all debt will be paid. Information on debt acquired before the marriage must be included with financial disclosure.

Postmarital education

In the event that you or your fiancé are in school or plan to further your education during the marriage, financial arrangements should be discussed. Marital debts are those incurred for a valid marital purpose, which generally means that it benefits both parties; separate debts are those incurred for a nonmarital purpose. The court may consider whether the other spouse benefited substantially from a student loan by sharing in the increased income for a substantial period of time or received other benefits. Without a prenup, it would be up to a court to consider whether the debt is considered marital and how to allocate the debt.

It should also be noted that a spouse's direct or indirect contribution during the marriage towards the other spouse's development of enhanced earning capacity may be considered under the relevant law as a factor in determining equitable distribution.[7] A prenup can address how this type of debt will be handled during the marriage and in the event of divorce.

Household budget

Many couples find it useful to clarify how the marital budget will work. For example, how will each spouse's income be used to pay shared bills? Perhaps the couple wants to preserve a percentage of each person's income as separate property and pool the remaining earnings. In some cases, when there is a large disparity in incomes, the couple may decide that one person may allocate a percentage of earnings to that person's savings and agree that these funds will be considered separate property. A prenup can also address how major expenses will be handled (e.g., requiring joint consent for major expenses before they are incurred). This type of clause typically defines a major expense in terms of dollars, such as any expense in excess of $2,500 or other agreed-upon amount.

Estate planning

Prenups should be consistent with estate planning documents such as wills, trust documents, and beneficiary designations. Every state has laws setting forth rights of a surviving spouse if there is no will. These rights are usually known as a spouse's elective share because the surviving spouse can elect to take property other than what is stated in the will of the deceased spouse. The waiver or nonwaiver of election rights affects how property will be distributed at death and can impact what has been put in place to protect separate property and the deceased spouse's beneficiaries other than the surviving spouse. States take different approaches regarding the elective share, and your attorney can provide advice on relevant estate law and how the decision to waive or not to waive the elective share impacts your overall estate planning goals.

---

7. Ibid.

Confidentiality

Couples sometimes opt to include confidentiality clauses in their prenups to ensure that the process remains clear of interference from family and friends. Confidentiality clauses are meant to protect privacy. Confidentiality can be addressed in a number of ways. First, the clause can pertain to the agreement itself and whether its existence will be disclosed. It can also specify that the content of the agreement remains confidential. While this type of clause may serve to demonstrate the importance of confidentiality, it may be difficult to enforce such a clause.

Social media and lifestyle

In the age of technology, social media has become both a blessing and a curse. Applications like Facebook, Twitter, Instagram, LinkedIn, and blogs have the ability to connect people who would have never otherwise met or allow old acquaintances to reconnect. On the other hand, these applications have the unique ability to invade privacy and cause harm.

To guard against disparagement, harm, and "social media drama," couples have chosen to include provisions in their prenup to address the agreed-upon use of social media. A clause can be included to stipulate what types of pictures or posts may be made, if any. In this way, potentially damaging posts can be prohibited. With these clauses, each person agrees that online posts will not be disseminated without prior written consent.

The type of information that may be protected includes information about the other person's personal and business activities, legal and business affairs, health, and sexual activities. These clauses can prohibit the electronic dissemination of photographs, videos, emails, or texts about or from the other person. For example, a (future) wife may want to authorize which photos of her become public domain on the (future) husband's Facebook or Instagram page, or the parties may want to agree that intimate marital details shall remain in the marriage and not be posted online. Some couples agree to nix social media entirely, agreeing instead to not maintain any active social media presence. These clauses, like confidentiality clauses, may be difficult to enforce. Some couples consider a financial penalty as a way of putting meaning into the clauses.

Pets

The person who brings a pet into the relationship may want to specify the custody and care of that pet. Likewise, the other person may want to ensure that the pet will remain the responsibility of the original pet owner or have an agreement on the ability to spend time with the pet. It is not uncommon for couples to agree on a visitation schedule or custody arrangement of a pet in the event the marriage ends.

Creating a safety net (cash reserve)

Most couples want to ensure that each person is taken care of financially, no matter what happens. The couple can create a comprehensive plan in the prenup that allows for an agreed-upon amount to be placed in a savings account for one or both of the spouses (see the section entitled "Household budget" on page 35). Building a cash reserve like this is often used when couples have a disproportionate balance of income.

State and international laws

Consider whether there may be a move to or from another state or country in the future, and then discuss this with your lawyer. Each state and country has its own set of laws regarding prenups. If you know that a move is possible, consult with counsel in the anticipated state or country to determine if your agreement would be considered valid and binding in that state or country. You may not know in advance about a future move; in that case, once a move is known, consult with appropriate counsel to review the prenup and determine whether it would be considered valid.

Sunset clause

Sunset clauses vary depending on personal circumstances. In general, they are not very common. Some sunset clauses provide that the prenup will expire after a certain number of years of marriage. Another type of sunset clause phases out the prenup over time. For example, the division of property and/or maintenance changes when certain milestones in the marriage are met, such as 10 years, 15 years, or 20 years. At each of the stages, more of the prenup becomes void, or more of the property becomes marital, until the last stage when the prenup is entirely phased out. Other sunset clauses phase out certain provisions while continuing to protect separate property or specified income and assets, even after the agreed-upon expiration date.

Challenges to the agreement/resolution of disputes

The agreement may contain a provision that neither of the parties will make an application in any court or forum for modifications of any of the terms of the agreement, or to set aside or rescind any of the terms of the agreement. In this type of clause, to the extent that any law permits a party to make such an application, the parties waive that right.

A related provision addresses what happens if such an action is commenced or if one party seeks to obtain anything beyond what he/she is entitled to receive pursuant to the agreement. This type of provision typically addresses responsibility for payment of attorneys' fees as a result of such action and the obligations attributable to bringing such an action.

Future disputes are sometimes addressed in another type of clause in which the parties agree to first attempt to reconcile a dispute by direct negotiation or by using a neutral mediator or collaborative lawyer before instituting a court action. Arbitration is sometimes considered to decide a specific, designated issue. While arbitration is an alternative to the courtroom, it is generally more similar to the courtroom than mediation. The effects of a decision about resolution of disputes should be understood before a decision is made about including such a clause in the prenup.

Items excluded from a prenup

State laws restrict what can and cannot be included in prenups. Your attorney can advise you as to the law of your state. Here is a list of topics that may not be allowed and/or be enforceable:

- Decisions about the custody and parenting access/visitation of the children or child support where a court has the final say in custody and parenting access/visitation based on a "best interest of the child" standard with several factors considered[8]
- Decisions about the religious upbringing of children
- Clauses considered to promote divorce
- Waiver of counsel fees
- Clauses promoting behavior that is illegal and/or against public policy
- Waivers of maintenance[9]

---

8. The needs of future children and what may be in their best interest may be difficult to predict at the time of the prenup, and clauses providing for custody and parenting access/visitation may not be enforceable if the court makes a determination that the pertinent clauses are not in the best interest of the child or if this type of clause is prohibited.

9. Some states prohibit or look down on waivers of maintenance and limit the ability to waive temporary or permanent maintenance rights. Some states, such as New York, allow it; however, relevant law provides that an agreement regarding maintenance must be "fair and reasonable at the time of the making of the agreement" and "not unconscionable at the time of entry of the final judgment" (NY DRL 236 B(3)).

The term "gray divorce" has recently come into use as a way of describing a divorce for older couples. Does this mean that we now have to use the term "gray prenup"? Somehow, that does not seem right. I prefer the term "platinum prenup." Platinum connotes stability and a strong foundation. Older couples may have different priorities and expectations. Platinum seems a fitting term because, frankly, it is more attractive than gray.

A platinum prenup, as used here, represents the possibilities of a new life while protecting the elements essential to both individuals coming to the union. In light of life expectancies and increased ways to maintain good health, the possibility of second and third marriages becomes more likely.

A later-in-life marriage presents different challenges and opportunities. A platinum prenup is a smart way to make a financial plan together. It also can help to maintain strong family connections by creating a plan for the future that honors prior family members. That means talking about goals for children from a prior marriage and how to implement plans towards those goals. It could also include plans for health care coverage and discussing what happens to retirement savings and income. In the next section, you will find issues to consider for a later-in-life marriage.

Platinum checklist

The following considerations will help you obtain a clear understanding of how prenups can be used.

RESIDENCE

Where will you live, and what will happen to each of the residences?

_____

_____

_____

How will expenses for the residence(s) be paid?

_____

_____

_____

Will you buy a new residence together?   ❑ Yes   ❑ No

If yes, how will the title to this residence be held?

_____

_____

_____

What happens to the new residence upon death or divorce?

_____

_____

_____

If you are living in a residence owned by one of the parties (purchased prior to the marriage), will there be a right to remain in the residence upon the owner's death? If so, for how long, and how will the carrying costs be paid?

_____

_____

_____

RETIREMENT AND SAVINGS

What will happen to retirement assets and savings acquired prior to and during the marriage?

_____

_____

What plans and benefits are available, including survivor benefits?

_____

_____

_____

What are the government benefits, and when will they be received?

_____

_____

_____

Is there already an agreement and/or judgment in place that must be considered?   ❏ Yes   ❏ No

Will there be shared savings?   ❏ Yes   ❏ No

What needs to be done to protect your goals in addition to the prenup (e.g., confirm how your retirement plan works and its beneficiary designations, confirm title/ownership of accounts, or describe what happens upon death in estate planning documents)? (See "Estate Planning" on page 44.)

_____

_____

_____

OTHER ASSETS AND LIABILITIES

What will happen to assets and liabilities acquired before marriage (other than the residence(s), retirement assets, and savings)?

_____

_____

_____

What will happen to assets and liabilities acquired during the marriage?

_____

_____

_____

Will there be limits placed on the incurrence of debts/expenses?   ❑ Yes   ❑ No

WORK

What are the plans for work/retirement?

_____

_____

_____

What is the income, and how will it be used?

_____

_____

_____

BUSINESS

Is there an interest in a business?　❑ Yes　❑ No

If yes, does the business generate income?　❑ Yes　❑ No

How is the income dispersed?

_____

_____

_____

Are there liabilities associated with the business?　❑ Yes　❑ No

Will the value of the business and/or appreciation of the business be allocated to your future spouse?　❑ Yes　❑ No

Does the business own real property?　❑ Yes　❑ No

HEALTH CARE COVERAGE

What is the current health care coverage, and will there be any changes?

_____

_____

_____

Is there long-term care insurance in place?　❑ Yes　❑ No

ESTATE PLANNING

What estate planning documents are currently in place (e.g., will, power of attorney, healthcare proxy, and/or living will)?

_____

_____

_____

What estate planning needs to be done to reflect future goals?

_____

_____

_____

What are the current beneficiary designations on assets, and do they need to be changed or reaffirmed?

_____

_____

_____

Will there be a waiver of the spouse's rights in the other's estate, or will both spouses choose not to waive their rights?

_____

_____

_____

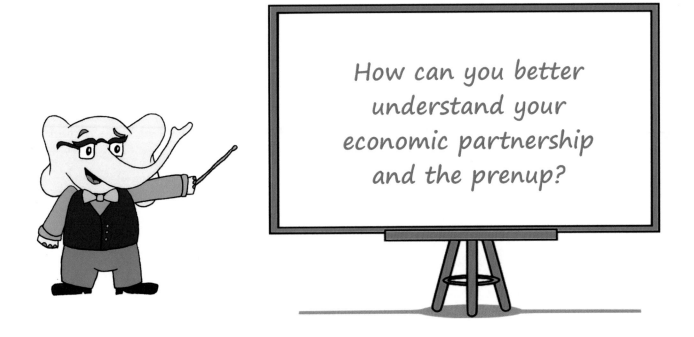

I have seen an increase in couples requesting prenups. Many look at a prenup as a way of taking an active role in the financial aspect of their marriage. In some cases, people are marrying later in life, which means that they likely have had more time to work and accumulate assets. Younger couples seek the protection of a prenup because of the security it brings in knowing how things will work during the marriage.

Times have changed, and couples today understand the importance of the economic partnership aspect of marriage. Applying the term "economic partnership" to a marriage may stir up various assumptions and feelings. However, ignoring the economic aspect of the marriage is unrealistic and does not help to build trust in the relationship.

Marriage is a union between individuals, and that union stems beyond the metaphorical sense. Even if you and your fiancé are looking to keep the bulk of your finances separate, an agreement can be used to clarify the details to ensure that your goals are met. There will undoubtedly be situations that need to be handled together, even when finances are kept separate.

An economic partnership means that you and your fiancé have an understanding of your respective financial situations and a plan to address assets, income, and debt. Couples may have their own unique philosophy on money and spending, and that's normal. Some couples find it difficult to have an open discussion about the financial reality before the marriage, especially when there is an imbalance in these assets coming into the marriage. Once the information is shared, the couple usually becomes more comfortable as the discussions progress. This approach is focused on working as a team and recognizing the value that each person brings to the marriage.

As you have seen throughout this chapter, a prenup gives you and your fiancé a way to address issues that may not yet have come into the relationship. When you sign a prenup, you're entering into a promise with your fiancé about how your marriage will operate and what each party is contributing. This can mean financial contribution to the household expenses, time spent for childcare and upkeep of the house, and anything else you may choose to include. While the wedding signifies your promise to stand beside one another and enter into a lifelong commitment, a prenup can actually help to provide a roadmap to a healthy, lifelong relationship.

CHAPTER 5

Prenups and Process

Make an informed choice about your attorney, and decide how you will negotiate the prenup.

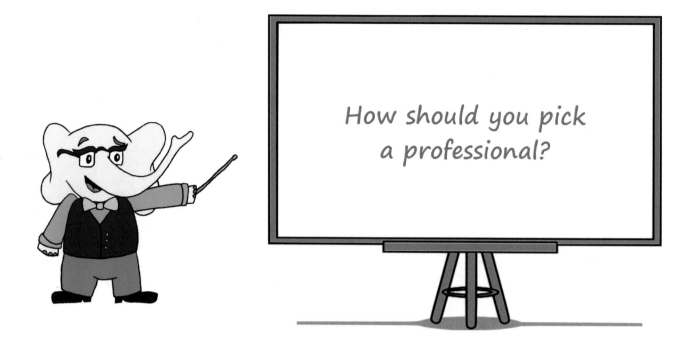

What should be on your short list for selecting an attorney? This is an extremely important decision that should be made with great care. It can affect how the negotiations take place as well as the effectiveness of the prenup document.

Considerations for choosing an attorney

Here is a list of things to look for when choosing an attorney:

- **Practice area:** What is the level of the attorney's expertise in drafting and negotiating prenups? What type of special training/knowledge does that attorney have? People usually feel more comfortable working with an attorney who knows the field well rather than with a general practitioner. The attorney should be competent in the specific area of prenups.

- **Personality and professional demeanor:** Is the attorney's approach consistent with how you would like to conduct the negotiations? Find someone with whom you feel comfortable. Is he/she client-focused and respectful of your goals and priorities? You will be sharing financial and personal information and negotiating sensitive issues, so the chemistry you have with the attorney is important.

- **Accessibility:** Will the attorney have enough time to devote to your case? How much time will the attorney need to produce the draft agreement once you have agreed upon the terms?

- **Communication/promptness:** Take into account the method of contact you require (e.g., email, phone, or in-person meetings). Also consider how long it may take the attorney to return communications to you.

- **Location:** Think of how far you are willing to travel to the attorney's office and whether the attorney charges for travel time.

- **Consultation:** A consultation should help you to clarify the effects of having or not having a prenup. You will come away with a better understanding of what needs to be done and when.

- **Size of practice/office:** Will the attorney handle all aspects of your matter, or will support staff or other attorneys be assisting?

- **Price:** Keep in mind that a variety of factors will affect an attorney's rate, such as the level of professional experience and the geographical area of the practice. Rates and an estimate of cost are usually discussed at the first meeting.

Working with an experienced professional can help you determine what may work best in terms of establishing a framework for the negotiations. A consultation with an experienced family law or matrimonial attorney will help you determine whether the attorney is a good match for your situation.

A professional who has seen a variety of clients may be able to offer practical considerations and options that facilitate arriving at a durable, enforceable agreement.

If you find yourself worried about bringing up the concept of a prenup, or if you want to understand how the agreement works, meeting with a professional will help you understand the mechanics and possibilities of the prenup as well as how to begin productive conversations.

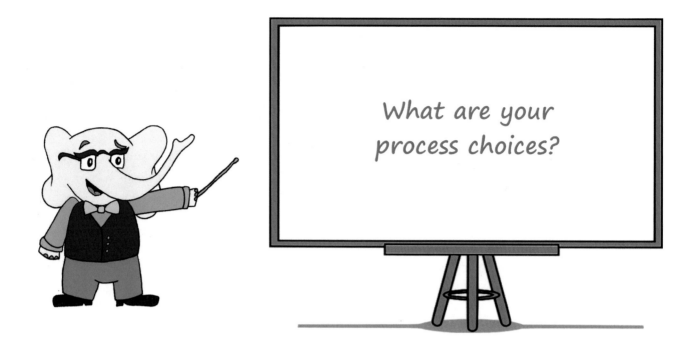

How you arrive at the prenup is just as important as the document itself. Process choices include collaborative law, mediation, and traditional representation by a family law attorney experienced in out-of-court, settlement-based negotiations. Each process will have the same objective, though the path taken to reach that objective will be slightly different. Also, the tone of the negotiations can be greatly affected by the process choice and structure of the negotiations.

The goal of any process should be to create a safe and dignified environment and to reach a balanced and respectful agreement.

Traditional route

You may choose a traditional route of representation based upon fair standards for a mutually satisfying agreement. This usually means that you and your fiancé would be represented by your own independent counsel. You and your attorney work together, focusing on your goals and priorities. Your attorney provides you with an understanding of relevant law and how it might impact the prenup. Your attorney will also review possible issues to be addressed. A draft term sheet is developed for review and discussion with you. This term sheet is then used to begin the negotiations. The prenup process will consist of meetings/discussions between the attorneys before you and your fiancé agree to the final product. The attorneys should be experienced in family law and, in particular, prenups.

Collaborative law

You can also work with a specially trained collaborative lawyer to advise you on relevant law and to help you negotiate the agreement. These attorneys are trained to solve problems and negotiate in a nonadversarial way. There is an agreement at the outset about how the negotiations will take place. The process involves working with lawyers in cooperative and respectful ways towards an agreement that meets the needs of both parties. The development of the prenup and the negotiations themselves take place during four-way conferences, as opposed to the traditional route where the lawyer is speaking for his/her client. Collaborative lawyers are accustomed to working productively with everyone in the same room and not allowing strong emotions to trigger positional bargaining. The focus in collaborative law is for an optimal result for both parties. It encourages an open environment and full disclosure from the parties.

Mediation

In this process, you and your fiancé work together with a neutral third party to arrive at the terms of your prenup. The mediator works as a facilitator to help clarify the parties' goals. The mediator structures the exchange of information and the negotiation. The role of the mediator is also to help frame concerns and keep the discussions productive. Once you arrive at an agreement, the mediator drafts a memorandum of the terms, which is called a "memorandum of understanding."

The mediator may also draft the agreement if he/she is an attorney. It is strongly recommended that you each retain an independent attorney to provide advice and counsel during this process and to review the agreement. This is an extremely important element when it comes to prenups. As a neutral party, the mediator does not represent the interests of either party. Your attorney will help to ensure that you understand the relevant law and that the agreement is binding in your jurisdiction. The importance of independent counsel is also reviewed in Chapter 9, Validity, on page 73.

What happens next?

Once you've chosen your attorney and the right process for you, it is now time to discuss the next steps with your attorney. The following timeline provides a sense of how you arrive at the final agreement.

Prenup timeline: from meeting your attorney to signing the final agreement

Consultation

Financial information prep

Meeting: financial review

Discuss goals with your fiancé

Prepare and review term sheet with your attorney

Draft agreement (prepared by attorney)

Continue discussions with your fiancé

Fine-tune and finalize the agreement (done with attorneys)

Congrats! It's time to sign your prenup!

The timeline can be modified to meet your own situation. It is intended to give you a general idea of how the process works and the steps that are involved.

Prenup timeline: a further look

The timeline on page 53 gives a sample of the process. The following expands on that timeline with some more information on what goes on during the process.

Consultation

The consultation on a prenup will usually begin with a determination of goals and priorities, including how best to involve your fiancé in the discussions. Next, applicable law and the requirements for a valid prenup will be reviewed as well as a checklist of possible subject areas for inclusion. After that, unique issues that you would like to address will be discussed. At the end of the meeting, an action plan for what happens next will be developed.

Financial information prep and review

Before your next meeting, prepare your financial information so that separate and marital property and debt may be identified and properly addressed in the agreement. Provisions about how the household budget will work may be included, depending on the couple's preference. Plans about income earned during the marriage also need to be reviewed. Depending on your situation, this may take more than one meeting.

Discussion of goals with your fiancé

At this point, the process is underway, and discussions with your fiancé have begun. Your fiancé's early involvement creates cooperation rather than positional thinking.

Preparation and review of the term sheet

A term sheet will be developed with the main terms of the proposed prenup. From a psychological standpoint, it is preferable to use a simple term sheet to confirm agreement on key issues before moving to the full agreement. It will allow for inclusion of your fiancé and avoid unnecessary legal fees for drafting a document that has not been agreed upon.

Negotiations and drafting of the agreement

Once your fiancé retains counsel, an introductory call will usually take place to discuss how the attorneys will proceed. Subsequent to the call, a term sheet will probably be circulated. Your fiancé's attorney will review the terms with him/her. After that, there may be some back-and-forth negotiations with the details. Your attorney will then proceed to draft the agreement.

Continuing discussion with your fiancé

While the negotiations are going on, it is advised that you maintain an open line of communication with your fiancé about your goals and your new life together.

Finalization of the prenup

Once the negotiations are complete, you will sign the agreement. *Congratulations!*

CHAPTER 6

Bringing Up the Prenup

Set the stage for a productive negotiation.

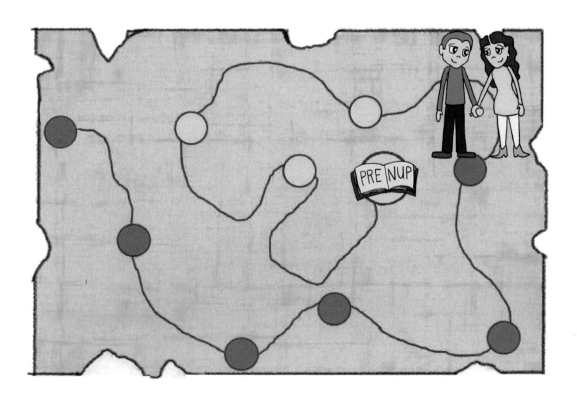

> How will you maintain dignity and respect during the negotiations?

How and when you talk about having a prenup is just as important as what goes into the prenup. Presenting a fully prepared agreement without any advance conversation can look like a "done deal" and may make the other person feel that they don't have a say in the relationship. For that reason, conversations leading up to a prenup need to leave room for both sides to be heard.

You know your fiancé best, and you need to think about the time and place to start these conversations. For example, it is not a good idea to start a conversation when there is time pressure about getting to work or attending an event. It is also usually best to avoid the end of the workweek when most people are tired. Pick a time when there is no pressing need to be somewhere else. Keep in mind that there should be several conversations before any decision is made. This alone should take some of the pressure off.

Basic ideas to help the path to a prenup go more smoothly

- **Consider the timing.** Start early! The sooner the conversation starts, the better. Try to pick a time when there are no deadlines or important events taking place. Set a date to follow up. Starting early helps alleviate the pressure and allows for thoughtful conversations. Conversations about money should be initiated before the marriage whether or not there will be a prenup. The time between getting engaged and the wedding day can be very emotional. You want to allow for time to have a dialogue with your fiancé. Conversations about financial goals and expectations are an important part of getting to know your future spouse. These conversations can take place before the word "prenup" is mentioned. Prenups that are drafted very close to the wedding can sometimes fall prey to a legal challenge, especially if one spouse was not involved until the last minute.

- **Clarify your own goals.** Understand why you want or need a prenup before speaking with your fiancé so that you are able to explain your reasons in an open and honest way. (See Appendix D, Goals, on page 111.) Once you clarify your goals, speak with an experienced attorney to determine how the prenup will accomplish those goals. A consultation with an experienced attorney will also help you understand the relevant law. Clarifying your goals and expectations will help you to speak more clearly with your fiancé.

- **Try your best to plan how you will talk about the prenup.** Feeling nervous about "the talk" is common, especially when you are not sure of your fiancé's thoughts on the topic. By organizing your thoughts in advance about why you want a prenup, it will help you express those thoughts.

- **Manage your emotional triggers.** Keep in mind that it is not only your fiancé who feels pressure; you are under pressure as well. Be aware of your own reactions to the initial conversations so that you can pace yourself. It may become clear that your fiancé also has ideas about the document. Listen to your fiancé's thoughts, and respond in a constructive way. When you are emotional, it sometimes inhibits the ability to respond well in a conversation. If you feel the tension building, take a break.

- **Be mindful of your fiancé.** Your fiancé may have different goals than you. You may be on the same page for many issues; however, there may be others upon which you do not initially agree or about which you may not have considered. That is okay. Accept that you may be in a different place and need to find a compromise. As you talk more about these issues, you will both have the chance to decide what is really important moving forward. Try to put yourself in your fiancé's shoes.

- **Ask yourself, "Why would my fiancé want to sign a prenup?"** You may not know the answer to this question. It is a question you can ask your fiancé as part of the discussion. You may find common ground by doing that. Be flexible, and listen to your fiancé. These conversations should be viewed as part of a larger picture of how you communicate with each other about finances and other issues. This should not be a one-sided document.

- **Share financial information.** Include information about your income, assets, and debts in your conversations about money. This should take place before you move to the conversation about the prenup document.

- **Present the topic before you present the document.** Once you have had conversations about money and your expectations for the economics of the relationship, you can start a discussion about the prenup. The topic should be presented before any document is drawn up.

- **Have a meaningful conversation.** Do not try to "sell" the prenup. There are no magic words. Talk about the prenup in terms of your broader goals. Keep the conversation as simple as possible. The concept of a prenup may be a new idea for your fiancé, and he/she may need some time to adjust. Stay flexible and understand that multiple conversations may be necessary to work out the details of the agreement.

- **Avoid a "take it or leave it" approach.** Handing your fiancé a multipage document without talking first may not be taken well—especially if it happens shortly before the wedding. As discussed in the section entitled "Preparation and review of the term sheet" on page 54, the term sheet provides a format that is easier to understand, has a better impact, and helps to create a feeling that you are on equal footing in the negotiations.

- **Adapt to the process.** As you go through the process, your ideas may change. Maybe something you initially thought was very important is no longer a big deal, or maybe you realize that there are a lot more details to consider. Your negotiations will be more effective if you keep an open mind as you work through the issues.

- **Avoid unsolicited advice.** Everyone is ready to give an opinion about what should be done. This is especially true of family members and friends. While others may have valuable input and advice, the conversation is best kept between the two of you and your respective attorneys. Be ready to address the concerns that are expressed in a meaningful way.

- **Monitor your tone.** Keep your tone even. Do not push too hard.

- **Don't get bogged down**. We all have certain "non-negotiables." If you find that you and your fiancé are having a hard time, table the issue and come back to it at a different time. You can also ask your attorney for advice about how to discuss the issue, or leave the issue for the attorneys to discuss. You are moving towards a happy event, and keeping your relationship on a healthy track is of paramount importance. Maintain your usual lifestyle with each other during the process.

These strategies should be adapted to your own style and how you feel your fiancé will be most comfortable in the process. An underestimated yet extremely valuable tool in the prenup process is a discussion *without* the word "prenup." Starting the process is less about the agreement and more about you, as a couple, talking about your relationship and your plans for the future. It may be helpful to prepare for the initial conversation. An outline might aid this preparation. If you and your fiancé are comfortable speaking about serious topics in a casual way, it might be beneficial to bring it up during some regular downtime. However, some people feel more comfortable in a scheduled, more formal setting.

Conversations about prenups are not easy, which is why so many people avoid them! If you approach these conversations with understanding and honesty, you and your fiancé will find yourselves in a great position for your wedding day and future life together.

CHAPTER 7

Client Interviews

Gain insight into the workings of a prenup negotiation.

This section is meant to give you a deeper perspective into others' prenup experience. The names and identifying facts have been changed to protect confidentiality. Any resemblance to real-life situations or people is coincidental.

What do clients say when they look back on their prenup experience?

Interview #1: Dan

How did the topic of a prenup first come up?

Friends of ours had tried to negotiate a prenup. That was the first time it came up.

What were your fiancée's initial thoughts?

My fiancée thought negatively about it. I let my fiancée know my viewpoint. We talked about this before I proposed. The first few times we discussed it were difficult because we had such different views.

What was the most difficult part?

The hardest part was the premise, not the contents. It was like a roller-coaster ride at the beginning. She wouldn't get an attorney at first, and that was difficult. I think it was hard to talk about what I wanted to accomplish. I was worried about my fiancée getting upset with me. Her reaction was that our relationship was not a business.

What helped you arrive at an agreement with your fiancée?

We kept talking. Talking it out helped. I tried not to convince her, but I asked her to research prenups. I think the most helpful part was when she got an attorney who helped her see that the agreement was fair for both of us and the way we kept talking until we both felt okay about it.

Looking back, would you have changed anything?

I think we could have talked more and sooner. I was nervous to show her what I have accumulated in my retirement accounts, and it also made me uncomfortable to talk about my income. I realize now that it actually felt good to share this information with her.

Did any member of your family help you? If so, how?

My family tried to stay out of it. My dad helped me work through the issues I needed to think about without giving me his opinion on whether the prenup was right or wrong for me. I really appreciated him being there for me without pushing me one way or the other.

How do you feel now that you have a signed agreement?

It feels good. I am relieved. I think it was a good exercise to go through my finances and expenses. I had never done that before in the way that we did for the prenup. Now, I think it's a good idea to make this kind of review on a yearly basis. It also feels good that my fiancée finally understands my goals and that, in the end, she was fine with the whole thing.

Interview #2: Antoinette

How did the topic of a prenup first come up?

We had talked about it. He mentioned it, but there wasn't any real communication, and then it went away. I thought maybe he wanted just a verbal agreement.

What were your fiancé's initial thoughts?

I could tell he was struggling with it. He was very emotional.

What was the most difficult part?

I wasn't upset at first. I was 100% on board with the idea because I knew it was important to him and his family. What made me livid was that it was sprung on me when he gave me the papers only two weeks before the wedding. That was the hardest part because we hadn't really talked about it in a long time. It was like a slap in the face. It seemed that he expected me to sign it without saying anything.

What helped you arrive at an agreement with your fiancé?

I didn't have a problem with the idea of a prenup. I was not okay with some of the terms. My attorney helped me calm down and work through it. She helped me to understand the terms, and we worked together on the terms that needed to be changed.

Looking back, would you have changed anything?

I would have changed the timing and the way I was given the agreement.

Did any family member help you? If so, how?

No, I didn't involve my family because I didn't want them to judge my fiancé. I relied on my attorney. When I first told my mom, I felt sick to my stomach. Before it was a reality, my parents were upset because they were together since high school and have a strong marriage. They were "old school" in a traditional way, but they stayed out of it for the most part. My mom never said anything. She comforted me and did not put in her two cents. When my father found out, he asked if I wanted to walk away. He stayed out of it and left the decision to me. I trusted my fiancé implicitly and knew he wasn't trying to stab me in the back.

How do you feel now that you have a signed agreement?

I feel fine now. It helped that we included a clause on putting in a safety reserve for me. My fiancé had a lot more money than I did, and we agreed that, after the wedding, I would set aside a percentage of my income each month. It made me feel equal in the relationship. I think we came up with a fair agreement, and I trust him. I am just so glad it's behind us. It did take me a couple of months to let it go. Now we're six months past the wedding, and I feel happy.

Interview #3: Jennifer

How did the topic of a prenup first come up?

This is a second marriage for both of us. It just came up in the conversation very naturally as something we both wanted.

What were your fiancé's initial thoughts?

We both wanted it from the beginning. We have both worked hard, we are pretty successful in our respective fields, and we wanted to preserve what we earned. We also felt that we wanted to keep our finances separate—even after the marriage.

What was the most difficult part?

Taking the time to put together the financial information. We are both very busy. Even though I understood that it was important to share our information, it was hard making time during the week. Once I set aside the time, it was easy to get the information prepared. My attorney helped by providing me with a list of what needed to get done.

What helped you arrive at the agreement with your fiancé?

We were in agreement on the general idea. Our attorneys were helpful in pointing out some of the details that needed to be addressed. We were lucky that we both chose attorneys who made sure things did not become hostile.

Looking back, would you have changed anything?

I think I would have started sooner, but it was impossible because my company was planning to move me, and I wanted to make sure where I would be living and that my fiancé could also secure employment.

Did any member of your family help you? If so, how?

No, we pretty much kept this private between the two of us. I did not feel that I needed any support, so I didn't discuss the prenup with my family.

How do you feel now that you have a signed agreement?

I feel relieved! I am glad we were able to get this done despite our busy schedules.

I hope that you found this section helpful. Most people find the process a useful one and see the value in sharing information about money and other issues before the marriage. There is usually a sense of relief in arriving at a signed agreement. All of these interviews demonstrate the importance of putting thought into bringing up the subject of a prenup.

Remember: How you talk about it is just as important as what goes into the prenup!

CHAPTER 8

Family Involvement in the Prenup Process

Balance your family's involvement in the process.

Over the years, clients have expressed different experiences about the role their family has played in the prenup process. Each family member brings different knowledge, experience, perspectives, and values into the equation. Families can provide valuable insight. Families may also focus on a particular position and lose sight of the big picture.

The couple is responsible for the ultimate decisions. For a negotiation to be successful, each person must feel that he/she is treated with respect and that his/her needs are being met. Effective negotiations can lead to positive outcomes and can strengthen relationships. The goal is to reach a mutually agreeable decision. Most people feel that, when their parents put too much pressure on them, it creates stress and results in the situation becoming more difficult.

Here are some suggestions for moms, dads, brothers, sisters, and other family members. Of course, every family is different, and what works for some families may not work for others.

Guidelines for family members involved in the prenup process

- **Be clear and positive.** If you feel that a prenup is needed, be clear about why, using everyday language to express your point of view. The reasons should be framed in a positive light. Treat your family member and his/her fiancé with respect. Express your feelings appropriately, knowing that a prenup can be a very emotional subject. Be aware of your emotions and how they can affect your behavior and your ability to communicate with your family member. For example, there can be very strong reasons for a family business or property bought by the family to stay in the family. Talk about why this is important to the family, the family history, and your values. Timing is critical. Make sure this issue is brought up well before the wedding.

- **Take a step back.** Once you have expressed your feelings about the prenup, take a step back and let the responsibility for taking action lie with your family member and his/her fiancé. If you are asked about your opinion, leave the ultimate decision about whether to enter into a prenup and the terms of the prenup to the parties. Helping your family member analyze the terms of the agreement, if you are asked, should be done in a constructive, noncritical way.

- **Avoid negative remarks.** Negative remarks about your son or daughter's fiancé will likely set the stage for strained relations with your new family member and your son or daughter.

- **Check your attitude and actions.** Avoid telling your family member what to do while keeping the lines of communication open so that your family member knows you are there for support. The attitude and tone you take become significant. Be open and honest while maintaining respect for both parties. Try to help your family member keep a balanced perspective. In the end, your attitude and actions can strengthen your relationship with your son or daughter.

- **Remain calm and breathe.** With your support, the family bond and your future family relations will be strengthened.

CHAPTER 9

Validity

Review the basic legal requirements.

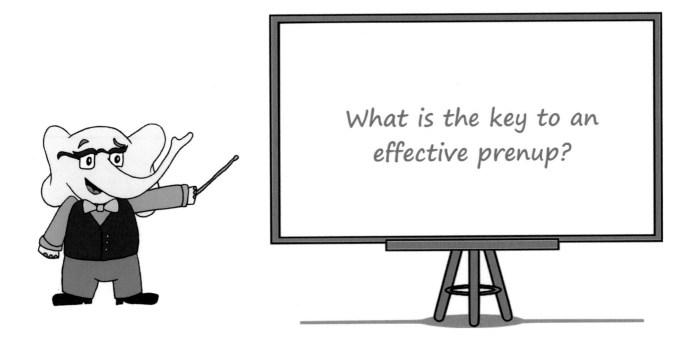

If love is the key to a happy marriage, what is the key to an effective prenup? A prenup establishes rights and responsibilities about finances and other issues. If done properly, this process can prevent future arguments over these issues. Basic contract rules apply to prenups. An agreement must be in writing and signed before a notary public.[10] The contract takes effect upon the marriage.

The contract is scrutinized under a unique set of procedural requirements (i.e., tests for substantive fairness both at the time of execution and at the time of enforcement) for the following reasons:

- The intimate relationship of the parties;

- The fact that children may be produced from the union; and

- The significant role the state has in regulating this relationship and in protecting spouses and children.

Because this contract can have long-term effects, there should be meaningful negotiations. The document needs to accurately reflect the couple's intentions and ensure that the requirements for an enforceable agreement are met.

The law surrounding prenups is very complex. At this time, most courts and legislative bodies in the United States generally view prenups as enforceable if they meet certain procedural requirements and are otherwise valid under general contract principles. Each state varies in its laws and in its decisions about what makes a fair agreement. A challenge to an agreement is done on a very fact-specific, case-by-case basis.

---

10. There have been some exceptions to this writing requirement; however, these were exceptions and not the rule. It is strongly advised to follow the rule.

In general, all agreements must be procedurally and substantively fair. That means the court will review the timing and execution of the document as well as the fairness of its contents. In determining whether an agreement is fair, basic principles of contract law (e.g., capacity, duress, fraud, and undue influence) are applied. The requirements covered in this chapter are recurring requirements regarding the validity throughout the United States that need to be considered.

Validity requirements

- **The writing:** The agreement must be in writing and signed by both parties with certain formalities. It must be signed before a witness (or witnesses, in some states) and have a proper acknowledgment (i.e., a notary signature). The agreement can be overturned if it is not properly executed.

- **Independent legal counsel:** This is a very important factor when considering challenges to a prenup. The lawyers help to ensure that both parties are making informed decisions about what goes into the prenup and that the agreement is drafted properly. In general, parties to a prenup must at least have the opportunity to consult with independent legal counsel.

- **Financial disclosure:** Full and complete disclosure is required in most states. Disclosure must be accurate and detailed. This can take time, and it is for the protection of both parties. The best way to make financial disclosure is to exchange current net worth statements, setting forth each person's assets, debts, liabilities, and income consistent with the language below. In some states, at least some degree of financial knowledge or at least the opportunity to obtain the knowledge is necessary. The level of financial disclosure varies among states. Some states permit the parties to waive disclosure. A material, fraudulent nondisclosure or failure to disclose a material fact may void all or part of the agreement. Generally speaking, here is a list of the documents exchanged as part of financial disclosure:

  - A statement of assets, debts, liabilities, and income, including a list of all financial accounts. It also includes a detailed list of real property and other residences that you own or have an interest in (e.g., home, cooperative apartment, rental property, vacation property, and timeshares) and debt and liabilities (e.g., mortgage, home equity line of credit, student loans, and credit card debt). (See Appendix C, Sample Financial Statement, on page 97, for a sample financial disclosure.)

  - Tax returns (e.g., W-2, 1099, K-1 forms)

  - Appraisal(s) or market analysis of real property

  - Information regarding business interests (e.g., name, type of entity, percentage, and value of the interest)

  - A list of personal property

Disclosure is usually coordinated with your attorney. Other items may need to be disclosed depending on the nature of your situation. In addition to exchanging information, any questions that may arise should be addressed.

- **Timing of execution:** A prenup must be signed before the marriage. The timing is an indication as to whether each person has considered the agreement thoroughly and signed it voluntarily. The closer to the marriage that the prenup is signed, the more likely a challenge will include this factor.

- **Requirement of marriage:** There must be a marriage subsequent to the execution of the agreement for it to be enforceable. If there is an annulment, a void marriage, or an unanticipated or prolonged delay in the marriage after the execution of the agreement, the agreement may be subject to a challenge.

- **Public policy limitations:** Some issues cannot be covered in a prenup because they are against public policy. As an example, limits on child support may be void. Provisions concerning the custody of children or a parenting schedule are normally not enforceable. A court will make its own review of what is in the best interest of the children. States vary in their approach regarding the waiver of spousal maintenance and counsel fees.

- **Fairness:** Some level of fairness is usually imposed for a prenup to be enforced. The degree of fairness that is required varies and may depend on the circumstances surrounding the agreement. An agreement may be overturned if it is unconscionable (i.e., extremely lopsided or favorable to only one party) at the time of execution, even if there has been full disclosure. Fairness factors considered include the objectives of the parties, the economic circumstances of the parties, the assets and liabilities of each party prior to the marriage, the existence of other family relationships and obligations, each party's income and earning capacity, the age and health of the parties, and the educational and professional background of each party. The analysis of fairness can be complex. For example, New York reviews the fairness of prenups at the time of signing and at the time of divorce.[11]

---

11. Spousal maintenance terms must be "fair and reasonable at the time of the making of the agreement and ... not unconscionable at the time of entry of final judgment" and a provision that waives or reduces support must not render a spouse "incapable of self-support and therefore likely to become a public charge." Domestic Relations Law Sec. 236B(3) & General Obligations Law Sec. 5-311. Additionally, a court may set aside a prenup if it deems it "manifestly unfair" to one spouse because of overreaching on the part of the other spouse. *Christian v. Christian,* 42 NY 2d 63, 72, 1977. In 2013, the New York courts made a pivotal ruling concerning prenups. In *Cioffi-Petrakis v. Petrakis,* the court set aside a prenup after finding evidence to suggest that the agreement was signed under duress and fraudulent circumstances. The court acknowledged that public policy favors individuals contracting on their own, but matrimonial issues are subject to additional scrutiny. The court also held that an agreement may be set aside if the party challenging it can demonstrate that "it was the product of fraud, duress or other inequitable conduct." *Cioffi-Petrakis v. Petrakis,* 103 AD3d 766 [2d Dept 2013].

CHAPTER 10

Hypothetical Case Reviews

Recognize the range of issues that can be addressed in a prenup.

My goal is to give you a basic understanding of prenups and provide you with a roadmap for going through the process. Because the attorneys are tasked with drafting the agreement and tailoring it to your needs, I have chosen not to include sample legal clauses because it would take away from the focus of this book. In the next section, I have provided hypothetical situations to help you see what a prenup can accomplish.

While reading through each of the following hypothetical case reviews, think about what types of issues you might want to include in your own agreement if you decide to enter into a prenup. The issues in each case are different because every couple is unique. Some couples limit a prenup to clarifying separate property acquired before the marriage; other couples want more comprehensive agreements concerning assets, debts, business interests, or other issues. These samples are created to demonstrate the breadth of issues that can be addressed through a prenup and to help you think about which issues may apply to your situation. In each case, there are many options for resolving the issues raised.

I have modified the facts and used the fictitious "John" and "Jane" as a model couple to protect confidentiality.

Hypothetical case review #1

OVERVIEW

John, age 35, has an MBA and is a wealth manager. He earns approximately $200,000 per year. He owns a house that his family helped him purchase. The house is worth approximately $600,000 and has a mortgage of $300,000. The couple has been living together in John's house for two years.

Jane, age 19, works as a personal trainer. She earns $15 per hour at a local health club. She also earns about $500 per week doing private personal training.

John is planning to install a new bathroom and kitchen in the house after the wedding. He wants to use some of the wedding gifts for that purpose. Jane is helping pick designs, colors, and appliances. Jane has put a great deal of work into the house and considers the house hers. John's family called him after he and Jane announced their engagement last year and told him to go see the family lawyer about doing a prenup to protect the house. John's mom and dad had given him $100,000 to buy the house four years ago. The house is in John's name only.

John and Jane talked about a prenup after the call from his parents. Jane told John that she would agree to enter into a prenup agreement. They never discussed the details except that the prenup had to do with the family's investment in the house. They never revisited the subject again during the year of their engagement. John procrastinated in taking any action because he was worried that the prenup would upset Jane, even though she said she was okay with it. He felt uncomfortable talking about his income and his savings with Jane.

About two months before the wedding, John went to his family's lawyer and asked him to draw up a prenup with the sole objective of protecting the family investment in the house. The lawyer drafted the agreement and delivered it to John without reviewing it with him. John gave the prenup directly to Jane exactly one month before the wedding. Jane did not receive any information on John's assets and liabilities with the document—only an appraisal for the home. Unbeknownst to John, John's lawyer included a clause requiring Jane to waive maintenance. The prenup did not address how payments towards John's mortgage from marital income would be treated.

Jane immediately hired a lawyer. When Jane's attorney called John's attorney, suggesting they discuss the terms, he stated that the prenup is a "take it or leave it" agreement. This was relayed to Jane, and she became extremely upset. She seriously thought about calling off the wedding. This was quite a change of events since Jane had always understood that John wanted to protect his family's investment and the retirement contributions he made prior to the marriage.

POSSIBLE QUESTIONS AND ISSUES

- Is the maintenance waiver fair?

- What are the options to protect John's interest in the house?

- How will the payments towards the mortgage be treated? Does Jane get a credit for payments made from marital income (i.e., income earned during the marriage)?

- If the wedding gifts or marital funds are used to make capital improvements to the house, how does that affect John's and Jane's property rights?

- What would make this agreement fairer to Jane?

- Does Jane still have the opportunity to change the agreement to suit her concerns?

Case #1 shows the importance of choosing an attorney who honors the relationship and who will facilitate a principled negotiation.

- John and Jane had discussed a prenup during their engagement, and Jane was agreeable to the idea. John delayed moving forward because he was worried about Jane's reaction to the agreement once she had it. Delivering the agreement in final form made it look like a "done deal," and it caused a bad reaction in Jane. Jane should have been involved earlier, and John's attorney should have reviewed all of the provisions with him so that he understood and agreed to all of the terms of the agreement.

- Whether a waiver of maintenance is fair depends on a number of factors, including but not limited to whether Jane had independent counsel, whether there was full financial disclosure prior to signing the agreement, and whether the waiver was fair and reasonable at the time of the agreement and not unconscionable at the time of the entry of the final judgment. In the above case, John's lawyer included a waiver of maintenance without first discussing it with John. John only cared about protecting his family's investment and his prior earnings. He wanted the house to eventually become Jane's with a credit to him for the equity in the property as of the marriage date.

SUMMARY

John and Jane were able to negotiate an agreement that protected John's interests as well as Jane's. Jane was able to negotiate changes to the agreement with the help of her attorney that addressed her desire to feel equal in the relationship. These terms omitted the waiver of maintenance and included setting aside a portion of Jane's finances each month that would be considered Jane's separate property.

Hypothetical case review #2

OVERVIEW

John, age 40, is a consultant in the finance industry. He earns $400,000 per year plus a substantial bonus. He bought his cooperative apartment at age 30, with funds inherited from his grandmother and with savings from employment. John recently refinanced the apartment, and the bank appraised it for $750,000. There is a $200,000 mortgage on the apartment, which is in John's name. He has also acquired retirement assets and stock options totaling $900,000. He has no student debt. John is going to marry Jane in six months.

Jane, age 26, is halfway through a postgraduate program in psychology. She may open her own practice someday. Jane earns approximately $20,000 per year as a teaching assistant. She has student debt of approximately $125,000. She has saved $20,000 working part time.

POSSIBLE QUESTIONS AND ISSUES

- John wants to clarify that the apartment is his separate property.

- What happens if the apartment is sold, and then John and Jane buy a home together with some of the proceeds?

- John wants to clarify that the retirement assets and stock options acquired before marriage are his separate property. Some of the stock options were granted and vested before the marriage, and some were granted but will vest after the marriage.

- What will happen to the appreciation of John's separate property?

- How will the mortgage on John's apartment be paid? Does Jane get a credit for marital funds used towards the paydown of the mortgage?

- How will Jane's student debt be paid?

- Jane will obtain her PhD during the marriage. Will Jane's enhanced earning capacity become a marital asset? Will John be entitled to share in the value of Jane's enhanced earning capacity?

- If Jane opens her own practice, will it be considered marital property?

- What happens to the separate and marital property in the event of divorce or in the event of John's or Jane's death?

Case #2 raises a number of issues that are different from Case #1:

- In this case, John wanted to protect his investments prior to the marriage. Both parties stressed the need for fairness and a feeling of equality in the marriage. Jane is about to begin her professional career, and she is not sure whether she will enter private practice or work for a public or private institution. The parties are extremely supportive of each other's career.

- After learning about applicable law from their respective counsel, John and Jane discuss the various available options. The goal of keeping property separate may be affected by many factors, including but not limited to relevant state law; title to the property; whether marital income is used for the carrying charges on separate property; whether there are additional contributions to an asset during the marriage and the source of those contributions (e.g., capital improvements and contributions from marital income to separate property); whether there is appreciation of the property during the marriage and whether the appreciation is active or passive; and whether the documents related to property are consistent with the intentions of the parties.

SUMMARY

By consulting with their attorneys and talking with each other, John and Jane became clearer on their priorities and developed an agreement that was unique to their situation. John and Jane entered into an agreement that protected John's separate property and identified property that would be considered Jane's separate property. The agreement also addressed how the paydown of John's mortgage would be treated and how the household budget would work. In addition, the agreement addressed whether John would have any interest or claim to the value of Jane's enhanced earning capacity. The agreement included provisions about how Jane's student debt would be paid and whether John would have any obligation towards that debt. In this case, John and Jane also considered whether to include sunset provisions regarding the distribution of certain property.

Hypothetical case review #3

OVERVIEW

John and Jane have been dating for over five years and have lived together for the past two of those years. They are both financially stable and have high-paying jobs. Since they have moved in together, they have been very budget conscious and split all common expenses in half including, but not necessarily limited to, rent and/ or mortgage and carrying charges and utilities. John and Jane take care of their personal expenses, such as the cost of medical insurance, clothes, and hobbies. The groceries are itemized so that each of them only pays for the items they actually use/consume. They plan on adhering to the same plan once they are married. John plans on proposing to Jane within the next year, and the couple anticipates that the wedding won't happen for about two years after that. John and Jane would like to start a family in the future but have not had any discussions about it.

POSSIBLE QUESTIONS AND ISSUES

- If the couple maintains separate incomes and is splitting the household budget equally, why would they want a prenup?

- Although this couple is splitting expenses, do they plan on keeping all accounts separate?

- Moving forward, will it be easier to continue to split everything down the middle, or will one party take over payments for certain things and the other party handle others?

- Does the couple want to confirm their agreement in writing?

- Is the couple interested in setting aside a portion of their earnings into a joint account for special circumstances or specific expenses?

- How will retirement and/or investment assets be affected without a written agreement?

- Does either party anticipate taking significant time away from work to care for future children?

- What will happen if the couple purchases property together?

- Without an agreement, will their state law dictate a different result in the event of a divorce or upon death than their stated intentions?

SUMMARY

When a couple's relationship is running smoothly, it can sometimes be hard to consider the benefits of a prenup or to think about "what if" scenarios. After all, if there is a good system, why worry about it? The "cross that bridge when you get to it" mentality in this scenario can lead to problems if there is no agreement, which may lead to unintended results.

Although the couple currently splits all of their expenses down the middle, what will happen to the household budget if either John or Jane is out of work for a period of time to care for future children or has experienced an involuntary/voluntary termination of employment? Additionally, would John and Jane like to have any money pooled into a joint account? Do John and Jane understand what happens to contributions to retirement/investment assets with and without an agreement?

Currently, John and Jane know that they would like to start a family at some point in the future. Prenup discussions would be a good opportunity for the couple to think about how the dynamics may change once children are in the household. The couple may want to think about how they will protect each other and the children in the event of a breakup of the relationship or upon death.

Hypothetical case review #4

OVERVIEW

John, age 70, and Jane, age 57, are getting married in one year. John has retired and earns income from his pension and from Social Security benefits. He has substantial retirement assets and investments, which generate sufficient income to support his current lifestyle. John has no debt. Jane has her own marketing business and earns approximately $150,000 per year. Jane does not want to retire for at least seven to 10 more years. This is a second marriage for both. John has three children from his first marriage (ages 30, 33, and 35). Jane has two children from her first marriage (ages 25 and 27). Jane is repaying student loans on behalf of her children. She also has some credit card debt. John and Jane each own their own home. John has a house in the suburbs that has no mortgage. Jane has an apartment in the city with a mortgage and common charges. John wants to preserve his home (or at least the equity in his home) and his retirement assets for his children. Jane also wants to preserve her apartment and retirement assets for her children. The couple would like to preserve both homes for a while and eventually move into Jane's apartment in the city.

POSSIBLE QUESTIONS AND ISSUES

- How can John and Jane protect their children from prior marriages?

- Will the title to the residences change upon marriage?

- How will assets be divided upon death? Upon divorce?

- Should Jane's business be valued? Is Jane's business separate property? What if the business appreciates during the marriage?

- How will Jane's debt be treated (i.e., the loans she took on behalf of her children)?

- How will the household budget work after the marriage? How will John and Jane contribute to household expenses?

- Will Jane continue to contribute to her retirement after marriage? If so, will these contributions be considered separate property?

- John has several antiques and valuable works of art. Jane has jewelry that has sentimental as well as monetary value. How will John and Jane make sure their children receive these items?

- If John and Jane move to Jane's apartment and Jane predeceases John, will John have to vacate the apartment upon Jane's death?

- Will there be changes to the current health care coverage? If so, how will the coverage be paid?

- What estate planning should John and Jane do to ensure that their intentions are carried out?

SUMMARY

John and Jane can certainly protect the assets they acquired before the marriage for their children. John and Jane will each prepare a statement of net worth and other relevant financial disclosure to ensure that all of the issues concerning their property and debt are addressed. Their respective lawyers will assist them in understanding what would happen if they change title to the property and will review the importance of beneficiary designations that are consistent with their wishes.

The value of Jane's business and Jane's intentions regarding her business should be discussed. The prenup will clearly identify separate assets and liabilities and describe what will happen. The prenup can also provide how income earned during the marriage will be treated. For example, a portion of John's income can pay the carrying costs of his residence, and a portion of Jane's income can pay her carrying costs and separate debt. There are other options as well for payment of these expenses.

Since Jane plans on continuing to work and saving for her retirement, the agreement can include a clause providing for Jane to do so. Since John is concerned that Jane's children may ask him to vacate her apartment in the event she predeceases him, a provision can be included giving John the time he feels he would need and to address how expenses for the apartment will be paid upon Jane's death.

Working together, John and Jane can agree on the best health care options available, and agree on a fair arrangement for sharing the cost of the coverage and how unreimbursed expenses will be paid. John and Jane should each consult with independent estate planning attorneys to ensure their estate plan reflects their goals.

Hypothetical case review #5

OVERVIEW

John and Jane are married. They have decided to move out of the city and purchase a home in the suburbs. They want to own the home jointly. In order to make the purchase in the neighborhood they want, Jane will use a portion of her savings that was acquired prior to the marriage. Even though the marriage is stable, Jane is uncomfortable dipping into her savings without protection.

POSSIBLE QUESTIONS AND ISSUES

- How can Jane make sure her savings continue to be identified as her separate property?
- How will the mortgage be paid?

- In the event of a sale, how will Jane's share of the proceeds be determined?

- If the property is owned jointly, how will Jane's interest be protected?

SUMMARY

In this case, even though the marriage is stable, Jane wants to protect her savings as separate property. A postnup can be drafted to address Jane's concerns and to address any concerns John may have. Both parties have spoken with their respective attorneys and understand that, once separate property is transferred to joint names, an issue may arise as to whether Jane's property remains separate. A written agreement can clarify the intentions of the parties and their intentions regarding what is Jane's separate property in the event of a separation, divorce, or Jane's death. The agreement can also address what happens in the event of a sale. For example, the parties can agree whether Jane gets a dollar-for-dollar credit or a pro-rata credit based upon her contribution in relation to the net proceeds of the sale. This is also an opportunity for John and Jane to discuss their individual contributions to the new property.

Hypothetical case review #6

OVERVIEW

John and Jane have been married for 20 years. They have two children (ages 9 and 11). John is an executive with a Fortune 500 company, earning approximately $500,000 per year plus bonuses and other executive compensation. Jane has a marketing degree; however, she is not currently working. She stayed home to raise the children. The couple owns their home, which has equity of about $900,000. There are also substantial retirement and other assets. Lately, the relationship has been rocky. Neither party wants to call it quits. Jane recently opened John's business credit card statement by mistake and discovered that John incurred substantial charges that are questionable. Jane loves John, but she questions whether she should trust him. John and Jane want to work on their relationship; however, Jane feels that she wants some security in case things do not work out.

POSSIBLE QUESTIONS AND ISSUES

- Can John and Jane enter into a postnup to reflect how assets and debt will be maintained and what would happen in the event of a divorce?

- What happens to the debt incurred by John, which is unrelated to his business or to the household?

- How will Jane's and John's needs be met in the event of divorce?

- Should the agreement include child custody and support terms?
- How will the value of marital property be determined in the event of divorce?

SUMMARY

John and Jane can enter into a postnup that addresses what will happen at this point in time and what will happen in the event of a divorce with respect to their assets and debt. They can decide whether the allocation of their property is equal or whether it will be shared in some other ratio. The agreement can and should address how and when property will be valued in the event of a divorce. One way that John and Jane can address the personal debt incurred on John's business credit card is by providing a credit to Jane or a lump-sum payment to her in an agreed-upon amount. The negotiations surrounding this issue in particular should be geared towards the future and preserving the relationship, if that is what the couple wants. The couple can address support for Jane in the agreement or state that it will be addressed upon the happening of certain events (e.g., a divorce action being commenced). Child support and custody terms should not be included if the divorce is not imminent. The agreement should clearly indicate which rights are reserved for determination at a later date. During this process, couples sometimes decide to divorce. The agreement could then be modified to reflect that decision and include custody, support, and other terms.

Hypothetical case review #7

OVERVIEW

Jane began dating John about three years ago while he was in law school. John put himself through law school by taking out student loans. Jane is an artist and a designer and is quite successful in an interior design business, which she started several years ago with a partner. John has now been out of law school for about two years, has passed the bar exam, and is working full time for a firm. He currently owes more than $200,000 in student loans for college and law school combined, with his monthly payments totaling more than $2,000. John and Jane currently live separately but just got engaged about two months ago. John plans on moving into Jane's house. Jane has about $500,000 equity in the property and has a mortgage of approximately $200,000.

POSSIBLE QUESTIONS AND ISSUES

- How will John's student loan payments be paid during the marriage? Upon divorce?
- Will John be making mortgage payments? Will John be added to the mortgage obligation?

- Will John or Jane be entitled to maintenance if he/she gives up his/her job and stays home to raise any future children, or will the couple's rights on this issue be reserved?

- Will title to Jane's house remain in Jane's name?

- What is Jane's ownership interest in the business? Is there a partnership agreement for Jane's business? What are Jane's expectations about ownership of the business?

SUMMARY

In this situation, John and Jane are both bringing assets and debt into the marriage. John is entering the marriage with his law license and substantial student loan debt. A prenup can address how the student loans will be paid as well as what happens to this debt in the event of divorce or death. Jane comes to the marriage owning a business and a home with a mortgage. John is moving into the home. Jane may want to protect her business and make sure that the house remains her own separate property.

A prenup can identify the business and home as Jane's separate property and what happens to the appreciation and/or debt related to the business. It can also address whether John will be contributing to the mortgage payments. If marital income is being used towards the mortgage, the agreement should address whether John gets a credit for such payments. An agreement can also address what happens if Jane sells the house and uses the proceeds to buy a new residence. The couple can decide whether they want to address equitable distribution of marital property or defer decisions on that issue.

Finally, while Jane's and John's income is unclear from the hypothetical, the couple may want to address their respective contributions to the household budget (in addition to payments towards Jane's house) and decide whether this issue will be addressed in the prenup. The couple should consider whether they want to include provisions regarding maintenance or reserve their rights for a future determination of this issue.

Common questions raised by the hypothetical case reviews

I hope the above scenarios helped broaden your scope of options to be considered in your own prenup, if appropriate. These examples can also show you how diverse these situations can be and that there are a variety of legal, financial, and other issues to address. Experienced, independent legal counsel should always be involved in negotiating and creating these agreements.

Here are some questions to consider:

- Are you adequately protected under the agreement in light of your unique circumstances?

- What statutes govern prenups in your state of residency, and how have these statutes been followed?

- How does your state of residency treat income, a pension, 401(k) and/or other retirement assets, gifts, inheritances, and other assets generally when acquired during the marriage? Does your agreement adequately reflect this topic?

- What is your attorney's anticipated role in the process of creating these agreements?

- Does your agreement address your intentions/assumptions regarding property and debt in the event of divorce?

- Will there be changes to the agreement based upon the number of years of the marriage?

- Are there estate planning issues related to the agreement?

- Will the agreement include lifestyle issues? (These provisions are meant to memorialize behavior and do not necessarily have legal consequences.)

Conclusion

The stories in this book show that a prenup represents
an opportunity to begin marriage with a clear
sense of each other's values and priorities.

Working on a prenup can also help to establish clarity about
your financial relationship. When the process works well,
it involves many aspects, such as gaining knowledge about
relevant law and its impact on your marriage, effective
communication, engaged listening, and recognizing and
understanding your emotions and those of your future spouse.

How you go about the process can deepen your connection
and build trust. I hope you are able to use this book to
make your process more productive and meaningful.

I wish you much happiness in your marriage
as you build your life together!

APPENDIX A

No-Nups (or Cohabitation Agreements)

When a couple does not intend to marry, a no-nup (or cohabitation agreement) can be used. The no-nup identifies each person's property and rights and sets forth each person's financial obligations. It is similar to a prenup in that it establishes what will happen to assets if the couple separates. Cohabitants have successfully asserted rights using this type of contract.

An existing will may not necessarily protect property rights and should be used in conjunction with an agreement, beneficiary designations, and other documents that reflect how the property should pass. A will alone should not be relied upon as it can be revoked, or it may be ineffective as to certain property if the title or beneficiary designations are not consistent with the will. A valid agreement can only be modified or revoked by a writing signed by both parties. All relevant documents regarding assets and debt should be reviewed by an attorney to determine whether the parties' intentions are met.

Cohabitation without a marriage has become more popular as social mores have changed. More women and men are delaying marriage to pursue an education, a career, and personal goals. A no-nup (or cohabitation agreement) is an important tool in protecting yourself and your assets when you do not choose to marry because you do not have the same rights and responsibilities that come with marriage. Laws relating to marital property do not apply to an unmarried cohabitant. A no-nup is created to set forth rights and obligations of the parties when they do not plan to marry. Not all rights and protections that come with marriage will necessarily be protected by a no-nup.

The issues and questions that can be addressed in a no-nup[12] include:

- How will you treat property that each party separately owns?[13]
- What will happen to property acquired during the nonmarital cohabitation if the parties later marry?
- How will property be divided if the relationship breaks down?

---

12. There are numerous other issues that can and should be addressed by a no-nup, depending on the circumstances of the parties and their goals and values. As with a prenup, experienced, independent counsel should be used in creating these documents.

13. The law regarding transfers of ownership of property must be reviewed to determine the effect of a transfer of title to property.

- How will household and other bills be paid?

- Will the parties execute wills naming each other as beneficiaries? Are there other estate planning issues related to the agreement?

- Will the parties name each other as beneficiaries on retirement assets and/or life insurance policies?

- What state laws will apply?

- Is there a possibility that there may be a move to another state or country?

- As with any agreement, your interests must be protected by both the form and substance of the agreement.[14] The law concerning what would happen without such an agreement must also be considered.

Here are some ways to talk about a no-nup with your partner:

- The agreement should be brought up as a positive way to address your needs and concerns and those of your partner. Listen to your partner and respond to his/her questions, concerns, or goals.

- This conversation can be part of a larger discussion about management of finances and how each person can feel more secure moving forward.

- More than one discussion is usually needed. Try to find a time when neither partner is under a time pressure.

- Developing a plan works best when it is a cooperative effort. Make sure that each person's concerns are included when brainstorming how the plan for moving forward will be carried out.

- As with the prenup, the no-nup may be used as an opportunity to clarify and understand each other's intentions regarding the relationship and how the couple might work together to build financial security and promote trust in the relationship.

---

14. See Chapter 9, Validity, on page 73, regarding writing requirements for valid agreements.

APPENDIX B

Postnups

A postnup is an agreement or contract made after a marriage that addresses the distribution of property (including property acquired before and after the marriage) as well as debt. It may also address the amount and duration of maintenance, custody and support of children, and other issues upon separation and death. (Whether the inclusion of provisions for custody and child support is appropriate should be discussed with an attorney.) A postnup can include testamentary provisions or a waiver of any right to elect against the provisions of a will. This agreement becomes an important part of the married couple's estate plan, and it should be consistent with the will and other estate planning documents.

Postnups are now widely accepted in the United States; however, they are not recognized in every state, so it is best to consult with an experienced family law or matrimonial attorney. In general, there is a strong public policy in favor of individuals resolving their own family disputes.

Couples sometimes consider creating a postnup under the following circumstances:

- There is a major negative or positive change to the couple's financial situation that may require a change in the couple's plans, and the couple wishes to memorialize a new plan.

- There is an infidelity or other trust issue that arises, and the couple wants to stay together with the security of having an agreement in place.

- The couple wants to acquire a business or property together and clarify ownership rights in the property. In other words, one or both members of the couple may want to use property acquired before the marriage to make a purchase during the marriage and want to preserve his/her rights in this property.

The following factors are usually required for a valid postnup:

- It must be in writing.

- It must be executed voluntarily.

- There must be full and/or fair disclosure prior to the time of execution.

- It must not be unconscionable.

- It must be executed and acknowledged in the same manner required for a deed to be recorded.

- Other considerations may vary depending on your state. The courts will normally consider whether each person was represented by independent counsel or had the opportunity to seek advice and counsel from an independent attorney.

Here are some ways to talk about a postnup with your spouse:

- The agreement should be brought up as a positive way to address your needs or concerns and those of your spouse. Listen to your spouse and respond to his/her questions, concerns, or goals.

- The conversation can be part of a larger discussion about family financial planning. It can also be a way to work on the marriage while removing any concerns about what will happen financially.

- More than one discussion is usually needed. Try to find a time when neither you nor your spouse is under a time pressure.

- Just as with the prenup, the postnup may be used as an opportunity to clarify and understand the family finances, work together on a plan for moving forward, promote a feeling of equality, and build trust in the marriage.

APPENDIX C

Sample Financial Statement

This financial statement is for *illustrative and informational purposes only*. Although this may help you better understand the type of information that will be needed when drafting your prenup, the categories listed here may not be exhaustive for your purposes.

BACKGROUND INFORMATION

Name: _____

Address: _____

Date of birth: _____

Anticipated wedding date: _____

Do you or your fiancé have children from a prior relationship/marriage? ❑ Yes ❑ No

If yes, list names and ages of children: _____

_____

Where do you plan to reside? _____

Your occupation: _____

Fiancé's name: _____

Fiancé's address: _____

Fiancé's date of birth: _____

Fiancé's occupation: _____

Supplemental information: _____

_____

_____

EXPENSES

This information may not necessarily be included in your prenup. It depends on how detailed you would like to be about the household spending plan.

Provide monthly amounts for all responses.

HOUSING

Do you rent?　❑ Yes　❑ No　　If yes, rent: _____

Do you own?　❑ Yes　❑ No　　If yes, mortgage amount and amortization: _____

_____

Real estate taxes: _____

Co-op/condominium charges: _____

Total Housing: _____

UTILITIES

Fuel oil: _____

Gas: _____

Electricity: _____

Water: _____

Total Utilities: _____

FOOD

Groceries: _____

Dining out: _____

School lunches: _____

Total Food: _____

HOUSEHOLD

Babysitter: _____

Housekeeper/maid: _____

Repairs: _____

Furniture, furnishings, housewares: _____

Appliances: _____

Sanitation/carting: _____

Gardening/landscaping: _____

Snow removal: _____

Other: _____

Total Household: _____

CLOTHING (ANTICIPATED EXPENSES)

Total Clothing: _____

INSURANCE

Life: _____

Homeowner's/renter's: _____

Fire, theft, liability: _____

Automotive: _____

Umbrella policy: _____

Medical: _____

Dental: _____

Optical: _____

Disability: _____

Worker's compensation: _____

Other: _____

Total Insurance: _____

UNREIMBURSED MEDICAL

Medical: _____

Dental: _____

Optical: _____

Pharmaceutical: _____

Surgical, nursing, hospital: _____

Other: _____

Total Unreimbursed Medical: _____

AUTOMOTIVE

Year: _____ Make: _____ Personal/business: _____

Year: _____ Make: _____ Personal/business: _____

Payments: _____

Gas, oil, repairs: _____

Parking/tolls: _____

Total Automotive: _____

RECREATIONAL

Fitness clubs/country clubs: _____

Movies: _____

Other: _____

Total Recreational: _____

INCOME TAXES

Federal: _____

State: _____

City: _____

Social Security and Medicare: _____

Total Income Taxes: _____

EDUCATIONAL EXPENSES (CHILDREN)

The following expenses relate to children from a prior marriage or relationship. If this section does not apply to you, skip to the next section entitled "Educational expenses (parties)."

Nursery/preschool: _____

Primary/secondary: _____

College: _____

Postgraduate: _____

Religious instruction: _____

School transportation: _____

School supplies/books: _____

Tutoring: _____

School events: _____

Other _____

Total Educational Expenses (Children): _____

EDUCATIONAL EXPENSES (PARTIES)

The following expenses relate to the existing and/or anticipated debt/expenses of the parties:

College: _____

Postgraduate: _____

Total Educational Expenses (Parties): _____

MISCELLANEOUS

_____

_____

TOTAL: $_____ USD

_____

GROSS INCOME (STATE SOURCE OF INCOME AND ANNUAL AMOUNT)

Salary or wages: _____

Weekly deductions:

- Federal tax: _____

- State tax: _____

- Local tax: _____

- Social Security: _____

- Medicare: _____

- Other: _____

Number of dependents: _____

Bonuses, commissions, fringe benefits: _____

Partnership, royalties, sale of assets: _____

Dividends and interest: _____

Real estate (income only): _____

Trust, profit-sharing, annuities: _____

Pension (income only): _____

Awards, prizes, grants: _____

Bequests, legacies, gifts: _____

Income from other sources (e.g., alimony and child support): _____

Public assistance: _____

Disability: _____

Other: _____

TOTAL: $_____ USD

ASSETS (STATE WHETHER HELD JOINTLY)

Because this is for *illustrative* purposes, each account type listed only includes space for one individual account. You may have numerous accounts that need to be listed.

Cash account(s):

- Location: _____
- Account number: _____
- Title holder: _____
- Date opened: _____
- Source of funds: _____
- Balance: _____

Checking account(s):

- Location: _____
- Account number: _____
- Title holder: _____
- Date opened: _____
- Source of funds: _____
- Balance: _____

SAMPLE FINANCIAL STATEMENT

Savings account(s):

- Location: _____
- Account number: _____
- Title holder: _____
- Date opened: _____
- Source of funds: _____
- Balance: _____

Security deposits and earnest money:

- Location: _____
- Account number: _____
- Title holder: _____
- Type of deposit: _____
- Date opened: _____
- Source of funds: _____
- Current value: _____

Stocks, options, commodities:

- Location: _____
- Title holder: _____
- Description: _____
- Source of funds: _____
- Date of acquisition: _____
- Original price or value: _____
- Current value: _____

Bonds, notes, mortgages:

- Location: _____

- Title holder: _____
- Description: _____
- Source of funds: _____
- Date of acquisition: _____
- Original price or value: _____
- Current value: _____

Trusts:

- Location: _____
- Title owner: _____
- Description: _____
- Source of funds: _____
- Date of acquisition: _____
- Original price or value: _____
- Amount of unpaid liens: _____
- Current value: _____

Loans to others and accounts receivable:

- Debtor: _____
- Original amount of loan or debt: _____
- Source of funds: _____
- Date payment due: _____
- Current amount due: _____

Value of interest in any business:

- Name of business: _____
- Your capital contribution: _____
- Percentage interest: _____

SAMPLE FINANCIAL STATEMENT

- Date of acquisition: _____
- Original price or value: _____
- Source of funds: _____
- Method of valuation: _____
- Other relevant information: _____
- Current net worth of business: _____

Cash surrender of life insurance:

- Insurer's name: _____
- Name of insured: _____
- Policy number: _____
- Face amount of policy: _____
- Policy owner: _____
- Date of acquisition: _____
- Source of funds: _____
- Current cash surrender value: _____

Vehicles:

- Description: _____
- Title owner: _____
- Date of acquisition: _____
- Original price or value: _____
- Source of funds: _____
- Amount of current lien paid: _____
- Current fair market value: _____

Real estate:

- Description: _____

- Title owner: _____
- Date of acquisition: _____
- Original price or value: _____
- Source of funds: _____
- Amount of unpaid mortgage or lien: _____
- Current fair market value: _____

Supplemental information:

_____

_____

_____

_____

TOTAL: $_____ USD

_____

LIABILITIES

Accounts payable:

- Name and address of creditor: _____
- Debtor: _____
- Amount of original debt: _____
- Date of incurring debt: _____
- Purpose: _____
- Monthly or other periodic payments: _____
- Amount of current debt: _____

Notes payable:

- Name and address of note holder: _____

SAMPLE FINANCIAL STATEMENT

- Debtor: _____

- Amount of original debt: _____

- Date of incurring debt: _____

- Purpose: _____

- Monthly or other periodic payments: _____

- Amount of current debt: _____

Installment accounts payable (security agreements, chattel mortgages):

- Name and address of creditor: _____

- Debtor: _____

- Amount of original debt: _____

- Date of incurring debt: _____

- Purpose: _____

- Monthly or other periodic payment: _____

- Amount of current debt: _____

Broker's margin accounts:

- Name and address of broker: _____

- Amount of original debt: _____

- Date of incurring debt: _____

- Purpose: _____

- Monthly or other periodic payment: _____

- Amount of current debt: _____

Mortgages payable on real estate:

- Name and address of mortgagee: _____

- Address of property mortgaged: _____

- Mortgagor(s): _____

- Original debt: _____

- Date of incurring debt: _____

- Monthly or other periodic payment: _____

- Maturity date: _____

- Amount of current debt: _____

Taxes payable:

- Description of tax: _____

- Amount of tax: _____

- Date due: _____

Loans on life insurance policies:

- Name and address of insurer: _____

- Amount of loan: _____

- Date incurred: _____

- Purpose: _____

- Name of borrower: _____

- Monthly or other periodic payment: _____

- Amount of current debt: _____

Other liabilities:

- Description: _____

- Name and address of creditor: _____

- Debtor: _____

- Original amount of debt: _____

- Date incurred: _____

- Purpose: _____

- Monthly or other periodic payment: _____

- Amount of current debt: _____

TOTAL: $_____ USD

YOUR NET WORTH = (YOUR TOTAL ASSETS) – (YOUR TOTAL LIABILITIES)

APPENDIX D

Goals

What are your goals when entering into a prenup?

The purpose of this appendix is to help you prioritize your goals in making a prenup with your fiancé. Prenups are tailored to your specific situation. A prenup can give insight into your and your fiancé's financial situation, your plan for the future, and how you plan to divide any responsibilities during the marriage. Once you evaluate what is most important to you, it will help the process to run more smoothly as the agreement is drafted by your attorney.

PRIORITIES (1 = not important; 5 = extremely important)	1	2	3	4	5
Protecting separate ownership of property acquired prior to marriage a) Home or apartment unit b) Business c) Retirement assets d) Other property					
Establishing responsibility for debt acquired prior to marriage (e.g., student loans or credit card debt) Addressing debt incurred during the marriage (e.g., will major purchases require joint consent?)					

PRIORITIES	1	2	3	4	5
Establishing whether income earned during the marriage will be considered marital or separate property					
Establishing whether contributions to retirement plans and other savings during the marriage will be marital or separate property					
Providing for children from a prior relationship					
Addressing maintenance/spousal support in the event of divorce					
Identifying estate planning needs Deciding whether each party will have rights to the other party's estate pursuant to state law or whether such rights will be waived					
Addressing use of social media					

APPENDIX E

Prenup Checklist

The following checklist reflects a quick reference for items to consider for your prenup. It is for reference purposes and may be modified to suit your unique situation.

Client name: _____

List your assets, liabilities, and income (refer to Appendix C, Sample Financial Statement, on page 97, for a more comprehensive worksheet): _____

_____

Agree upon what happens to your premarital property and postmarriage appreciation, gains, income, rentals, dividends, and proceeds of such property: _____

_____

Agree upon what happens to your postmarital property: _____

_____

Determine ownership of your marital residence and secondary homes in the event of death or divorce:_____

_____

Provide how premarital and postmarital debts will be paid:_____

_____

Discuss expectations of gifts and inheritances and how each will be treated: _____

_____

Discuss expectations of trusts either spouse receives or benefits from, before, or after marriage: ____

_____

Confirm the beneficiary of all 401(k), 403(b), profit-sharing, pension, IRA, and all other retirement plans, and state if such benefits will be divided: _____

_____

Clarify what will happen to each type of property, whether jointly or individually owned: _____

_____

Figure out alimony, maintenance, or spousal support, or provide for a waiver or property settlement instead of support (your attorney will advise you on your own state's law): _____

_____

Identify your estate planning needs (e.g., wills, trusts, elective share, powers of attorney, healthcare proxy, and/or living will): _____

_____

Identify medical, disability, life, or long-term care insurance coverage: _____

_____

Identify your respective attorneys: _____

_____

Determine what state's laws will apply and how your agreement will be affected by a move to another state (your attorney will advise you on this and help you to understand the law and its distinctions): _____

_____

About the Author

Deborah Hope Wayne is a collaborative attorney and mediator who dedicates her professional life to helping people negotiate family and divorce matters and resolve conflict without court intervention. She sits on the board of directors of the New York State Council for Divorce Mediation (NYSCDM) and is a founding member of the Academy of Professional Family Mediators (APFM). She is chair of the Accreditation Committee for NYSCDM. She is also a former member of the Board of the New York Association of Collaborative Professionals and is cochair of the committee for peer support and development for that organization. In addition, Ms. Wayne is a Certified Divorce Financial Analyst™.

Ms. Wayne codeveloped one of the first law school programs on collaborative practice in the United States and currently serves as Adjunct Professor of Collaborative Law at Pace University School of Law where she has taught for the past eight years. Ms. Wayne attended Boston University where she received a bachelor of arts cum laude; attended the University of Grenoble, Grenoble, France; and earned her law degree from Pace University School of Law. Ms. Wayne continued her study of negotiation at the Harvard Negotiation Insight Initiative in Cambridge, Massachusetts.

Ms. Wayne is an experienced divorce and family law attorney and mediator, and works as settlement counsel to help clients resolve disputes and negotiate agreements as an alternative to litigation. Her training in conflict resolution includes the following areas: prenups, high-conflict personalities, complex financial agreements, child-inclusive mediation, special-education needs, parent-teen conflict, and LGBT advocacy. Ms. Wayne is fluent in French and Spanish.

Other professional affiliations:

- Member of the International Academy of Collaborative Practitioners
- Mediator, roster for court-referred mediation cases for the Westchester Supreme Court, Westchester County, New York
- Member, Family & Divorce Mediation Council of Greater New York
- Founding member, Academy of Professional Family Mediators
- Facilitator, Center for Understanding in Conflict

Ms. Wayne has lectured on prenups, collaborative law, mediation, and conflict resolution at various institutions including St. John's University, Pace University School of Law, and Fordham Law School. She codeveloped and participated in the following programs:

- "Prenups, Postnups and No-nups: A Multi-Disciplinary Approach," Catalyst Conference, Association of Divorce Financial Professions and the Center for Mediation, New York, New York

- "Prenups, Postnups and No-nups: The Legal and Psychological Challenges for Mediators," New York State Council for Divorce Mediation, Buffalo, New York

- "Fear, Revenge & Anger: The Delicate Balance of Mediating Prenups & Postnups, An Intersection of Psychology and Law," Academy of Professional Family Mediators, San Diego, California

- "Domestic Violence and Collaborative Practice: the Complexity of Power in Relationships," Pace University School of Law, White Plains, New York, and New Jersey Collaborative Law Group

- "Legal Education and Collaborative Practice," International Academy of Collaborative Practitioners, Minneapolis, Minnesota

- "Collaborative Practice: The What and the How," New Rochelle Bar Association

- "Key Moments in a Collaborative Case: First Contacts with the Client and the Team," Office of Court Administration, New York State

For more information, please visit Ms. Wayne's website: www.deborahwaynelaw.com.

Deborah Hope Wayne, P.C., is located in Purchase, New York, and in New York City.